A USER'S GUIDE TO THE BIBLE

A User's Guide to the Bible

BIBLE STUDIES FOR GROWING
F A I T H

LYNNE MOBBERLEY DEMING

UNITED CHURCH PRESS
Cleveland, Ohio

United Church Press, Cleveland, Ohio 44115
© 1999 by United Church Press

Biblical quotations are from the New Revised Standard Version of the Bible,
© 1989 by the Division of Christian Education of the National Council of
the Churches of Christ in the U.S.A., and are used by permission.

Printed in the United States of America on acid-free paper

04 03 02 01 00 99   5 4 3 2 1

Library of Congress Cataloging-in-Publication Data

Deming, Lynne M.
    A user's guide to the Bible / Lynne Mobberley Deming.
        p.   cm. — (Insights : Bible studies for growing faith)
    ISBN 0-8298-1335-7 (pbk.)
    1. Bible Introductions. I. Title. II. Series: Insights
(Cleveland, Ohio)
    BS475.2.D45   1999
    220.6'1—dc21   99-32551
                                                           CIP

Contents

Introduction

A User's Guide to the Bible is just what the title indicates—a basic introduction to the Bible. In this study you will learn about the contents, date, and authorship of each of the biblical books. You will also learn how those particular sixty-six books came to be collected into a single volume, and how that volume came to be divided into chapters and verses. In addition, you will learn about basic Bible study tools and how to use them.

A User's Guide to the Bible is the first study book in a new series called *Insights: Bible Studies for Growing Faith*. The series grows out of an expressed need among UCC congregations for simple, short-term Bible studies that adults can use individually or in groups. The sessions in this study and in those that will follow in the Insights series are constructed so that an individual can read the information and stop at key points to think about its implications. Or a group can read the information collectively and pause at key points to discuss what they have read. The questions that are set off throughout the narrative are provided for this purpose. Good discussion questions are invaluable for any Bible study, and we have tried to provide thoughtful, thought-provoking ones in these studies.

Insights is not a book-by-book study of the Bible. As a rule, these studies will be thematic or topical. Upcoming topics include facing change, friendship, and spiritual disciplines. We will occasionally provide short-term studies on portions of Scripture, such as the Psalms or one of the Gospels.

We at United Church Press intend to publish one of these Bible studies approximately every six months. All studies will remain available for an extended period of time, so you can order them for whatever time frame is most convenient for you or your group.

We know that there is a hunger for more knowledge about the Bible, and we also know that hunger springs from a need to find meaning and direction in the complicated and complex lives we lead. Insights is our contribution toward feeding that hunger.

LYNNE MOBBERLEY DEMING, Publisher
United Church Press

A USER'S GUIDE TO THE BIBLE

ONE

Bible Ingredients

THE BIBLE'S TABLE OF CONTENTS

INTRODUCTION

Ecclesiastes 12:12 tells us, "Of making many books there is no end, and much study is a weariness of the flesh." Even though the Bible itself warns us against the dangers of too much study, Christians of all generations have been both fascinated and challenged by this complicated and multifaceted Book of books, the Bible. In today's session we will study the basics of what is in the Bible and learn something about how the sixty-six books found their way into the Bible's table of contents.

Often the word "canon" is used to describe the Bible's content. *Canon* is a Greek word that originally referred literally to a "measuring rod" or "stick." Later the word took on the figurative meaning of "standard" or "norm." So when "canon" is used to describe the contents of the Bible, it means the books that were determined, through a lengthy and complex process, to measure up to the standards of sacred literature. That process of decision making about what books were finally included in the biblical canon shows a fascinating intersection between divine revelation and human efforts.

In a recent research project to determine the role and authority of Scripture in the United Church of Christ, participants were asked whether they thought it was advisable to add books to or remove them from the existing biblical canon. The question was stated in this way: "Do you wish the Bible could be expanded to include more recent writings that were also inspired by God?" The answers to this question were interesting:

> Yes, definitely: 18 percent
> Yes, maybe: 18 percent
> Uncertain: 20 percent
> No, probably not: 21 percent
> No, definitely not: 23 percent

Much will undoubtedly be made of this question and its answer. But at the very least the response points out the need for further study and understanding of the concept of canon. We will return to this research question at the end of the session and ask whether your views have changed as a result of today's study.

If you are using this resource in a group, take a few minutes to discuss the question of whether adding books to the Bible is a good idea. What might a "yes" answer to the question mean? What might a "no" answer mean? How would you answer? Why?

THE BOOK OF HEZEKIAH

Among seminary students in introductory Bible classes, there is a joke that circulates about the book of Hezekiah. Of course, there is no book of Hezekiah in the Bible, but many people (including students of theology) could be convinced that it is there. And if it is there, it is probably among the historical books in the Old Testament. Many of the names of biblical books sound alike. If you are nervous about your biblical knowledge (or lack thereof), rest assured that many students entering seminary are dealing with the same issue.

Have you ever been concerned that your lack of biblical knowledge would cause you embarrassment? How would you assess your level of knowledge about the Bible?

THE BIBLE'S TABLE OF CONTENTS

The Bible is the sacred text of our Judeo-Christian heritage. The Old Testament, which is the legacy from the Jewish portion of our tradition, contains thirty-nine books and is divided into four main portions in our English versions:

1. The Torah, or Pentateuch—the first five books of the Bible
2. The historical books—the twelve books from Joshua through Esther
3. The wisdom literature—the five books from Job through Song of Solomon
4. The Prophets—the seventeen books from Isaiah through Malachi

The New Testament contains twenty-seven books and is divided into four main parts:

1. The four Gospels
2. The historical book of Acts

3. The twenty-one letters
4. The apocalyptic book of Revelation

Take a few moments now to look through the table of contents, or list of books, that appears in the front of your Bible. Familiarize yourself with the names of the various books. Do they all sound familiar? Was there a Hezekiah-type book on your list of biblical books that you now discover is not really there? Which books do you see on the list that you did not know were there?

Now let's take a few minutes to look further at the various categories just listed. Have a Bible handy so that you can page through the eight sections as they are described.

1. The Torah. This section is also called the Pentateuch, meaning "five books." In various places in the Scripture, this group of five books is called "the book of the law of Moses." We know the books of Genesis, Exodus, Leviticus, Numbers, and Deuteronomy existed as a separate collection at the time of Ezra (in the fourth century B.C.E.) because they are referred to in Nehemiah 8:1: "They told the scribe Ezra to bring the book of the law of Moses, which God had given to Israel." The leaders then read aloud from this collection as part of a festival celebration: "So they read from the book, from the law of God with interpretation" (Neh. 8:8). Next time the Scripture is read aloud in worship, remind yourself that this practice has a rich heritage that spans at least 2,500 years.

2. The Historical Books. As a group and individually, these books are less well known than the first five books.

These twelve books chronicle the history of the Israelite people from the time of Joshua (approximately 1400 B.C.E.) through the time of Ezra and Nehemiah (fourth century B.C.E.). Imagine the task of providing one thousand years' worth of history in such a relatively small number of words. As you page through this part of the Bible, you will notice that some books have what seems to be more than one chapter: you will see First and Second Samuel, First and Second Kings, and First and Second Chronicles. Each of these books was divided into two portions because of its unwieldy length.

3. *The Wisdom Literature.* As we move from Esther to Job, we move from historical writing to theological writing, from narrative to poetry. As you page through this section of the Bible, notice that the text is arranged mostly in poetry form rather than in prose. The wisdom literature consists of the books of Job, Proverbs, and Ecclesiastes, and portions of the Psalms; the Song of Solomon is included in this section because it is poetry.

4. *The Prophets.* The books from Isaiah to Malachi are mostly prophetic in nature. The first three books (Isaiah, Jeremiah, and Ezekiel) are commonly referred to as the major prophets; this designation comes strictly from their size and does not imply that their content is superior or somehow more important. The twelve minor prophets form most of the remainder of this section, along with the books of Daniel and Lamentations.

5. *The Gospels.* As you turn the page from the end of Malachi to the beginning of the Gospel of Matthew, you

are bridging a gap of approximately five or six hundred years. (Note: if the book of First Esdras follows Malachi in your Bible, see the section below on the Apocrypha.) The first four books in the New Testament are called Gospels, a word that derives from an Anglo-Saxon word (*godspell*) meaning "good news" or "good story." Each of the four Gospels tells the story of Jesus Christ in a different way and with a different emphasis. Reading the four Gospels is like looking at the story of Jesus through four different lenses. The basic story is the same, but each writer has a special emphasis and a unique approach.

6. *Acts.* The book of Acts is essentially a historical record that builds a bridge between the life of Jesus and the establishment of the early church. It was originally the second half of the Gospel of Luke, but it became separated at some point before the canon was established.

7. *The Letters.* Bible interpreters usually divide the letters into those written by Paul and those written by others. Thirteen of the letters are ascribed to Paul in their opening sections: Romans, First and Second Corinthians, Galatians, Ephesians, Philippians, Colossians, First and Second Thessalonians, First and Second Timothy, Titus, and Philemon. (Authorship of these letters will be discussed in session 4.) The rest of the letters were written by prominent teachers in the early church to keep in contact with newly established congregations.

8. *Revelation.* The letters are followed by the book of Revelation, which is classified as apocalyptic literature. The word "apocalyptic" means "unveiling" or "disclosure." Ap-

propriately then, the author of Revelation discloses in the book an imaginative description of the future of God's reign.

The Apocrypha. The Apocrypha is a collection of fifteen books that appear between the two testaments in some versions of the Bible. The word "apocrypha" means "hidden things" and designates in this case books that are informative but not recognized by the Protestant church or the tradition as part of the sacred Scriptures.

HOW WERE THE BOOKS OF THE BIBLE COLLECTED?

How were the sixty-six books collected into a single volume called the Bible? Who did the collecting? Who made the decisions? When and how did all this discernment take place? First of all, it is important to understand that this process of collection and compilation was an editorial process, somewhat like the process we use today to produce a book. Of course, our editorial process today usually takes less than five hundred years and involves fewer persons. We will take a closer look at the complete editorial process (chapters, verses, and related matters) in another session, but today we will examine the process used to decide which books were to become part of the canon. That process was similar to the process of deciding what chapters or essays might be included in an anthology. One very important similarity is that both processes involve people making decisions.

Think about the editorial process. With the others in your group, discuss what questions might be important to consider when deciding how to select a collection of essays to be included in a book. Act as a committee of persons established to put the book together, and suggest guidelines that might apply.

The exercise prompts us to think about what it might be like to make decisions about which books are appropriate to include in a collection and which ones are not appropriate. The process of deciding which books would be included in the Bible (sometimes called the closing of the canon) took place in two parts: Old Testament and New Testament. Since the two processes were very different and took place at different times, we will examine each process separately. Each process involved a series of issues and decisions similar to those you discussed in the exercise.

The Canon of the Old Testament

Earlier in today's lesson we spoke of a group of books called the Apocrypha, which are some of the books that were not eventually included in the canon. The Old Testament itself mentions other books that existed and were read and used by the Israelite community. Two examples are "the Book of the Wars of God" (Num. 21:14) and "the Book of Jashar" (Josh. 10:13). Although these books and others existed at one time, we have no indication of what happened to them after they were excluded from the canon of the Old Testament. The existence of these books shows that there was a process of decision making that included some books and excluded others.

The canonization of the Old Testament was an extended process that spanned at least five hundred years and consisted of at least three identifiable stages. The stages relate to the different kinds of literature found in the Old Testament.

1. *The Torah.* First, the Torah (the first five books of the Bible) was canonized. We know this decision was made by the time of Ezra (around 400–350 B.C.E.), since "the book of the law" is mentioned as a document that was read publicly at that time.

2. *The Prophetic Books.* Next, the prophetic books were added to the canon. That happened sometime between 450 B.C.E. (when the book of Malachi was written) and 200 B.C.E. The latter date is established by a quote in one of the apocryphal books that speaks of "the law and the prophets" as an established body of literature.

3. *The Writings.* The third stage in the canonization of the Old Testament concerns the Writings—the wisdom literature and much of the historical literature. This stage was a single event rather than a process. In 70 C.E. the Romans destroyed the city of Jerusalem, which threatened the very existence of Judaism and its traditions. In an effort to preserve the rich heritage of the faith, a group of rabbis met twenty years later at what was called the Council of Jamnia to make once-and-for-all decisions about what books were to be included in the canon of sacred literature. Although we do not have records of their proceedings, ancient writings indicate that the rabbis were

working with several guidelines when making these decisions.

- First, it was generally known that prophetic inspiration ceased at the time of Ezra. Therefore, since Ezra lived and worked in the fourth century B.C.E., no book written after that time could be accepted into the Old Testament canon.
- Second, the rabbis made every effort to maintain internal consistency among all the books that were included. Literature containing information that conflicted with previously established sacred texts was excluded.
- Third, any documents that were already in use and considered worthy by the community were included if they met the previous two criteria. This third guideline accounts for the inclusion of at least five books (Lamentations, Song of Solomon, Ruth, Ecclesiastes, and Esther) because they were already being read regularly at certain festivals.

Of course, this process was not exact or well documented. There were probably other guidelines of which scholars are not aware. What other guidelines can you imagine might have been used?

The Canon of the New Testament

The canonization process for the New Testament took place in at least four phases and lasted several hundred years.

- The first phase was the gathering of the four Gospels into a single collection. That occurred at the beginning of the second century. Paul's letters were also collected at that time, as 2 Peter 3:16 indicates: "Speaking of this as [Paul] does in all his letters. There are some things in them hard to understand, which the ignorant and unstable twist to their own destruction, as they do the other scriptures."
- The second phase took place during the period between 180 and 200 C.E. Official pronouncements during that time indicated that there was still dispute over the legitimacy of seven New Testament books: Hebrews, James, Second Peter, Second John, Third John, Jude, and Revelation. All other New Testament books were officially included by that time.
- During the third phase of the process (200–325 C.E.), the church father Origen indicated that he still had doubts about the status of James, Second Peter, Second John, Third John, and Jude.
- The fourth phase of the process took place between 325 and 400 C.E., during which time two or three official pronouncements listed all twenty-seven books that now comprise our New Testament. And the list has not changed since that time.

Guidelines used by the early church to make canon decisions included the following: acceptance and use of the book in the life of the church, a congruence with the traditional teachings of the church, and apostolic origin (it was written by or at least authorized by one of the apostles).

Now go back to the research question mentioned at the beginning of today's lesson: Do you wish the Bible could be expanded to include more recent writings that were also inspired by God? With what you now know about the canonization process—its complexity and duration—how would you now answer the question posed to the respondents? Do you wish the Bible's contents could be expanded to include other, more recent writings? Would additions like that be appropriate? Why, or why not?

Deciding which books should be included in the canon was only the first step in the creation of the Bible we use today. At the time of Jesus, the Scripture as used by the early Christians had no chapters, no verses, no spaces between words, and (in the case of the Hebrew Old Testament) no vowels. The long process of bringing the Bible to us involves many decisions by many people. Here is one example. How would you read the phrase that appears in the brackets? [nicestartinthecompetition] The scribes who worked with the Hebrew text to make it more user-friendly made important decisions about where the spaces between words should be located. We will learn more about this and related topics in the next session.

TWO

Bible Text

THE EDITORIAL PROCESS

INTRODUCTION

In the last lesson we looked at the various books in-cluded in the Old Testament and the New Testament and learned about the process of deciding which books should be included in the canon. That overview was the big pic-ture of how the books in the Bible were collected. During this lesson, we will be more specific, taking a look at how those scrolls were transformed into the Bible that we now have. That long process began with the creation of the Hebrew alphabet three thousand years ago.

The Hebrew alphabet contains twenty-two letters, some of which correspond to the letters of our alphabet in the way they sound. (For example, the second letter of the Hebrew alphabet is called *beth*, similar to our "b.") The Hebrew alphabet is different from ours in that it contains no vowels. We will examine what that means later in this lesson. Scholars have traced the Hebrew alphabet as far back as to the year 1000 B.C.E., the time of King David. Remember that David is credited with authorship of at least some of the psalms, and it is quite possible that he actually did this writing in what we now know as biblical Hebrew.

Before 1000 B.C.E., writing was done in pictures. This kind of writing is called "hieroglyphics." You have probably seen pictures of cave walls and monuments that contain hieroglyphics. In fact, early writing of manuscripts (the word "manuscript" means "written by hand") was done on items such as clay tablets, stones, animal skins, pottery, and papyrus. Writers most often used reeds and ink made from natural substances.

The original scrolls containing books of the Bible were written on papyrus. Papyrus consisted of sheets approximately 8 1/2 by 11 inches (like our standard page today) that were glued together into sheets that were thirty or thirty-five feet long. Unfortunately, no original Old Testament or New Testament manuscripts have survived until today. The original manuscripts were circulated and copied, and early scribes did not realize the value of the original manuscripts.

Talk with your group about the copying and circulating of manuscripts. How has the invention of photocopying changed the way we handle original documents?

GETTING THE PICTURE

Have you ever heard of the Dead Sea Scrolls? Their discovery was very important to biblical history. In 1947, archaeologists working in caves in the Judean desert unearthed a number of clay pots containing scrolls used by an early Christian community called the Essenes. The discovery was made in a place called Qumran. Before that time, the oldest available biblical manuscript came from the ninth century c.e. With the discovery of the Dead Sea scrolls that date changed to the third century b.c.e., one thousand years earlier. Still, however, the oldest surviving manuscripts were dated seven hundred years after the time of David. Imagine what can happen to a manuscript when it is copied (by hand) and recopied for seven hundred years.

Picture King David, three thousand years ago, writing psalms on papyrus shoots that were later glued together into larger sheets more than thirty feet long. What did these scrolls actually look like? The writing probably looked something like this:

galfehtotecnaigellaegdelpi
aciremafosetatsdetinuehtfo
rofcilbuperehtotdna
sdnatstihcihw
elbisividnidogrednunoitaneno
llarofecitsujdnaytrebilhtiw

This bunch of letters probably makes no sense to you. But would it make more sense if you knew that Hebrew was written and read from right to left? And there were no spaces between the words in original biblical Hebrew. Now can you read these words? If you discovered that this is the Pledge of Allegiance, you are doing the work of a Hebrew scribe.

THE WORK OF THE SCRIBES

The biblical text was copied and recopied in this form until sometime around 500 B.C.E.—that is, for five hundred years after the oldest portions were written. Around 500 B.C.E., a group of Hebrew scribes called the Masoretes (in Hebrew the name means "fence") decided that it was time to "fix" the text into one final form that could not be changed. This would be like writing a chapter of the book, running the spell check, and saving the file. The scribes were, according to their name, putting a fence around the text so that it would be predictable and unchanged from that time on.

> Like the rabbis who decided which books should be included in the canon of sacred scriptures, the Masoretes left no records of their work and their decisions. Try to imagine their reasons for placing this fence around the Old Testament.

Whatever their reasons, the accomplishments of these Masoretes made the Hebrew text more user-friendly. For instance, they marked the exact midpoint of each book in the Old Testament in terms of the number of letters each one contains (did you know that the midpoint of the book of Joshua is Josh. 13:26?). They calculated the midpoint of the Hebrew Old Testament to be Jeremiah 6:7 (the books in the Hebrew version of the Bible are in a different order from the way they appear in our English versions). You may think that is interesting but not terribly important, but the Hebrew text was read portion by portion on a regular schedule in worship services, and it was important to keep track of that schedule.

The work of the Masoretes also included such tasks as the following:

> Counting the number of letters in each biblical book
>
> Marking the *hapax legomena* (words that are used only once in the Old Testament)
>
> Counting the occurrences of divine names (such as God, Almighty)

Breaking the text into paragraphs (for easier reading during worship services)

Perhaps the most important task accomplished by these scribes was called "pointing." Originally, the Hebrew text consisted of consonants only, no vowels. You can imagine the confusion that might occur when the text contained no vowels. Take, for example, the word "STAR." How many different ways could the consonants "STR" be pronounced if you were not certain which vowel was involved?

STAR
STAIR
STARE
STIR
STORE
SATYR
SATIRE

You can probably think of other configurations. That was the task facing the Masoretes, but it was magnified by the number of words in the Hebrew Old Testament. Let's return to the Pledge of Allegiance that we read earlier, but this time we will look at the words without the vowels.

glfhttcngllgdlp
crmfsttsdtnhtf
sdntsthchwrfclbprhttdn
lbsvdndgrdnntnn
llrfctsjdnytrblhtw

Would you be able to identify this collection of consonants as the Pledge of Allegiance? How did these scribes move from "glfhttcngllgdlp" to "galfehtotecnaigellaegdelpi"? How did they know where to place which vowels? Remember that the text had been read aloud in worship services for hundreds of years. That oral tradition formed the basis of their decision making. That—and grammatical common sense. But you have an idea of the multitude of decisions and judgments that had to be made in the course of this human endeavor.

Once the decisions were made about which vowels were to be included, they were inserted as points, dots, and dashes that surrounded the consonants. That is why the process was called pointing. The scribes were guided by their reverence for the text as a sacred document that could not be altered in any way. Inserting vowels in between the consonants (as we did with "STR") was thought to be changing the text and was therefore not allowed. That is why a look at a Hebrew Old Testament today shows strings of Hebrew letters surrounded by dots and dashes over and under the letters.

> Some people are troubled by the idea that a particular verse could be translated more than one way, and so may have more than one meaning. Does this idea trouble you? How does the process described here affect your view of the Scripture?

Number Crunching

The process of putting a fence around the text took approximately eight hundred years. Beginning in the fifteenth century or so, when books began to be printed, scholars numbered the verses and chapters.

Think about trying to teach a Bible class using a translation in which the chapters and verses were not numbered. How could we identify which verse we were discussing? How could we ever talk about our favorite Bible verses? How would we identify the Twenty-third Psalm? We should be grateful to the scribes for doing this work on our behalf.

Making Decisions

At some point in this process, decisions were made about how the text should be divided into words, since in the original there were no spaces between the words. Recall the phrase nicestartinthecompetition, mentioned in the previous session. How did you read that phrase? Is it "nice start in the competition"? Or is it "nicest art in the competition"? The meaning of the phrase is very different, depending on how the words are divided. The Masoretes had to make similar, but much more important decisions as they worked.

Our English Bibles contain many instances that demonstrate this decision-making process. Find a Bible that contains notes about alternate translations (most do), and look up Psalm 44:4. The text reads as follows in most translations: "You are my King and my God; you command victories for Jacob." In this reading, it sounds as if the psalmist is praising God for God's work on behalf of Jacob, a metaphor for the people of Israel. But now look at the variant reading, usually indicated in a footnote. It says, "You are my King, O God; command victories for Jacob."

In this variant reading, it sounds as though the psalmist is asking (or ordering) God to act on behalf of the people.

So why does the text indicate that there is a variant reading? The two choices represent two possible ways to space the words. In this case, the scribes chose what seems to be the most logical spacing, the one that makes the language sound like a psalm of praise. However, either translation is appropriate from a grammatical point of view.

Sometimes a variant reading is included because one manuscript is written in a way that makes more sense than another. To date, more than five thousand New Testament manuscripts have been found, and scholars have used many of these manuscripts in order to provide the best possible translations.

Look up John 10:29, and check to see whether your translation contains a footnote about a variant reading for this verse. In this case, the original text reads: "What my Father has given me is greater than all else" (NRSV). But another manuscript reads as follows: "My Father who has given them to me is greater than all." That variant reading is given in a footnote because the New Revised Standard Version translators decided that the different reading may make better sense. It is important to remember that we do not have one right reading and one wrong reading. We have the benefit of the work of translators, who have provided options from which we can choose.

Look through the Bible, and note the many variant readings that are indicated in the footnotes. You can appreciate the complexity of the process used by the scribes and the many decisions they had to make along the way. From word spacing to addition of vowels to inclusion of chapter and verse numbers, the creation of the biblical text we use today was a human process to make the text more useful and more predictable. We would not want to make these kinds of decisions each time we open a Bible.

The recent research project mentioned in the previous lesson asked respondents to rate their agreement or disagreement with the following statement: The Bible was written by people inspired by God. More than 60 percent of respondents definitely agreed with this statement. Talk about this issue with your group. After today's lesson, how would you respond?

THREE

Bible Literature

DATES AND AUTHORSHIP (PART 1)

Introduction

Assigning dates and authors to biblical books is not an easy task, and much disagreement exists among scholars and students of the Bible. As we will see in today's lesson, most of the biblical books are compilations, or collections of earlier material that circulated either in oral form or in written form. For the historical books (Genesis through Second Chronicles), we must distinguish between the dates of the events portrayed in the books and the dates the books were actually written or compiled. And in the case of the prophetic books, we must distinguish between the time in which each prophet lived and worked and the time in which his writings were actually prepared and collected. So the process is very complicated, and dates and authorship can be determined in more than one way.

What you will read here is one opinion based on recent scholarship. But there are others. You would benefit from reading about other opinions in commentaries and other Bible study resources.

The Bible contains sixty-six books, and these books come in various shapes and sizes. We have books of history, prophetic literature, poetry of various kinds, proverbs, narratives, theological treatises, apocalypses, and letters, to name a few. The purpose of this lesson and the one that follows is to provide an overview of these various types and to provide some basic information about dates and authorship of the biblical books.

The Historical Books

The first historical books that we encounter as we open the Old Testament are the Law (Torah), or Pentateuch, the first five books of the Bible. We learned in another lesson that these books were the earliest to be canonized, or declared to be sacred texts. These books are Genesis, Exodus, Leviticus, Numbers, and Deuteronomy. Scholars and students thought for many years that Moses actually wrote these first five books, since they are called the books of Moses in the Hebrew and Christian traditions.

Look up John 7:19. What does that verse say about who wrote "the law," or Torah?

More recent scholarship has questioned the idea that Moses wrote the first five books of the Old Testament. Probably the most obvious problem is that the book of Deuteronomy reports the death of Moses. (Read Deut. 34:1–8.) In addition, the Pentateuch contains two different versions of a number of events. The best-known duplication is the story of the creation (Gen. 1 and Gen. 2). But there are other repetitions as well.

Look up the following verses, and note the duplication: Genesis 21:31 and Genesis 26:33.

If Moses did not actually write this material as it now exists, who did? The material is most likely a collection of previously written stories and accounts that were later combined into a series of books and then even later combined into the five books we have today. Theories abound as to the authorship of the Torah, but we will look at two main theories here. First, some scholars think that the final editing and collection were completed by the time of Samuel, about 1000 B.C.E. The second theory is often called the documentary hypothesis, which holds that the Pentateuch is a collection of four sources (called J, E, D, and P).

The J source was the earliest written (about 850 B.C.E.) and can be identified by the use of the word *Yahweh*, translated in most of our English versions as "Lord." The E source was written sometime around 700 B.C.E. and is identified by its use of the term *Elohim*, usually translated "God." The D source is the book of the Law that was found in the Temple during the time of King Josiah. You can read about this book in 2 Kings 22. The D source is mainly found in the books of Numbers and Deuteronomy. The P source is so called because it was contributed by a person or group for whom priestly matters were important. Most of the ritual language and text comes from this source (the first story of creation, the genealogies, and most of the book of Leviticus).

According to the documentary hypothesis, an editor put the Pentateuch together sometime around 400 B.C.E., using the four sources that were available and weaving them into the historical narrative that now exists. That history explains why and how the Israelite people were chosen by God to be the people of God, were sent into captivity in Egypt and then released, were given the law (Ten Commandments) on Mount Sinai, wandered in the wilderness for forty years, and finally found their way to the promised land of Canaan.

> The research survey mentioned previously asked whether respondents could recite any or all of the Ten Commandments. One out of five said he or she could recite all ten of the commandments. Almost half said they could recite most of the commandments, and one out of three could recite some of them. A few people responded that they could not name any. How would you respond to that question?

Page through the first five books of the Bible, and see whether you can identify any or all of these sources. And remember, the documentary hypothesis is, after all, only a hypothesis. No one really knows for certain how the Pentateuch was put together.

The book of Joshua, also a compilation from earlier sources, tells the story of the conquest of Canaan, the promised land. Just arriving in Canaan did not fulfill the promise made to Abraham (Gen. 12:1–3); the Israelites still needed to prevail over the inhabitants of Canaan in order to fulfill the promise. The author of Joshua combined a straightforward historical narrative (chaps. 1–12) with various public records of lists, genealogies, and other information into a single book. The process was completed about 650 B.C.E.

The same process was used to complete the book of Judges, which was actually compiled approximately 150 years before Joshua was completed (about 800 B.C.E.).

The book of Judges is the story of Israel's life after the conquest of Canaan. The people were organized into twelve tribes, loosely connected, and were constantly fending off attacks from neighboring peoples. Thirteen judges ruled over the land during this time; the most famous were Deborah, Gideon, and Samson.

> Read Judges 10:15–16. What is the main point the writer of Judges is trying to make?

The book of Ruth was also written about 800 B.C.E. Named after its main character, the book was probably based on an early story that circulated either in written form or in oral form. The message of the book deals with foreigners and attitudes toward them. That would be an appropriate theme during the time of the Judges. The character of Ruth is well known because of her loyalty to her mother-in-law, Naomi, but also because she was the great-grandmother of King David (read Ruth 4:13–22).

The books of First and Second Samuel were originally a single book, but were divided in half because of the length of the scroll. (The same is true for First and Second Kings, First and Second Chronicles, and Ezra and Nehemiah.) Although many people think Samuel was the author of the books of Samuel (that makes sense), he could not have been for the same reason that Moses could not have been the author of the Pentateuch. First Samuel 25 chronicles his death. Most of First and Second Samuel was probably part of a larger history that began with some of the book of Deuteronomy and included the books of

Samuel and Kings. This history, called the deuteronomistic history, was probably written in the sixth or seventh century B.C.E.

The books of Samuel chronicle the lives of Samuel, Saul, and David. This history is followed by a history of Solomon and the divided kingdoms in the books of First and Second Kings. The events described in Kings span four hundred years, from 961 until 561 B.C.E. Like Joshua, Judges, and the books of Samuel, the books of Kings were compiled from earlier sources.

> Look up 1 Kings 11:41 and 1Kings 14:19 to see examples of such earlier sources. Why do you suppose these other sources did not survive until today, whereas the biblical books have survived the test of time?

With the books of First and Second Chronicles begins another collection, which also includes the books of Ezra and Nehemiah. The books of Chronicles cover some of the same history as is found in First and Second Kings, but this author/editor wants to portray an idealized picture of that history in order to show that the Israelites were God's chosen people and David was their glorious and perfect king. (For example, the well-known incident of David and Bathsheba was omitted from the Chronicles account.) The author of Chronicles used the books of Samuel and Kings as sources, as well as other books that are no longer in existence.

> Look up 2 Chronicles 24:27; 27:7; and 33:18 for examples of other sources.

The books of Ezra and Nehemiah cover the period from 538 B.C.E. (the end of the Babylonian exile) through the ministry of Nehemiah, which lasted until about 398 B.C.E. Ezra and Nehemiah were scribes who took an active role in the restoration of Jerusalem and the worship life of the Hebrew people after they were released from Babylonian captivity. These books were compiled from various sources, including memoirs of Ezra and Nehemiah, and official documents and records.

The book of Esther was the product of an unknown writer during the Persian period. It tells the story of a Hebrew woman (Esther) who became the queen of the Persian king Artaxerxes and delivered the Hebrew people from bondage by that king. The story took place in 400 B.C.E., but the book was probably written around 200 B.C.E. It was written in part to explain the origin of the Jewish feast of Purim, celebrated annually even now to commemorate the story of Esther.

WISDOM LITERATURE

Turning the page from Esther to Job opens up a new chapter in biblical literature. We are moving from historical narrative into the literature of wisdom. The Old Testament wisdom literature, which occurs mostly in the form of poetry, encapsulates life lessons and morality and was passed along from teachers to students in the ancient world. The most well-known wisdom literature in the Bible is probably the book of Job. Written sometime around 400 or 350 B.C.E., Job addresses the question of suffering and why it happens to a person like Job, who is a moral and upright human being. Much of the book circulated in the oral tradition before it was written down.

The Psalms, although usually classified as wisdom literature, are a collection of songs that were used in the Jerusalem Temple in the postexilic period. Seventy-three of the psalms are ascribed to King David, and it is possible that some of them were actually written by him around the year 1000 B.C.E. The final collection appeared around 400 B.C.E. There are 150 individual psalms in the Psalter, and they are divided into five smaller collections, each ending with a doxology.

> The collections are Psalms 1–41; Psalms 42–72; Psalms 73–89; Psalms 90–106; and Psalms 107–50. Think about the doxology we often sing in our worship services. Now look up the last few verses in each of these collections to see the doxologies that close each section.

The psalms are often classified according to the way they were used in worship. Look up an example for each psalm type, and read all or part of that psalm aloud:

> Hymn (Ps. 8)
> Lament (Ps. 3)
> Thanksgiving (Ps. 63)
> Wisdom psalm (Ps. 1)
> Psalm of comfort (Ps. 23)

The book of Proverbs was authored by a group of sages who were associated with the king's court in ancient Israel. The sages also functioned as teachers, and proverbs were one way they could pass along their wisdom to their students. Parts of the book of Proverbs are attributed to various sages by name: Solomon (1:1), Agur (30:1), and Lemuel (31:1).

Page through the book of Proverbs, and notice how the form changes from narrative prose (chaps. 1–9) to poetry with short, pithy sayings (chaps. 10–31). The material in the later chapters is actually earlier in origin and more secular. The material in chapters 1–9 is more theological and was probably written at a later date. The whole collection first appeared after the return from Babylonian captivity (after 550 B.C.E.).

The book of Ecclesiastes was also written by a wisdom teacher, who identified himself only as Qoheleth (sometimes spelled Koheleth), or the preacher. The author told us a little about himself and his goal in writing the book: "Besides being wise, the Teacher also taught the people knowledge, weighing and studying and arranging many proverbs. The Teacher sought to find pleasing words, and he wrote words of truth plainly" (12:9–10). A scan of the contents of this book reveals how different it is in tone from the rest of the Scripture, and scholars have long puzzled about how and why this book was entered into the canon.

Read Ecclesiastes 1:1. What clue is there about why this book might have been included in the list of biblical books?

The goal of Ecclesiastes was to provide for future readers one person's view about the meaning of life. Like the book of Job, Ecclesiastes attempts to find meaning in the midst of a complex and seemingly chaotic world.

The Song of Solomon was written by an anonymous author who held Solomon in high esteem and wanted to attribute his work to the king. He actually mentioned Solomon on several occasions in the book (1:5 and 3:7, for example). The book is a collection of about twenty-five songs that were compiled by an author/editor sometime around 200 B.C.E. to be used as a songbook for weddings. Because it was written and/or compiled relatively late, translation is difficult because the vocabulary is different from that of most other Old Testament literature.

In the next session we will look at dates, authorship, and content of the Old Testament prophetic literature, and the books of the New Testament.

FOUR

Bible Literature

DATES AND AUTHORSHIP (PART 2)

INTRODUCTION

In the previous session we examined the Old Testament historical books and wisdom literature. In this lesson we will look at dates, authorship, and contents of the prophetic literature in the Old Testament, and all the books in the New Testament.

THE PROPHETIC LITERATURE

The writing of the prophetic literature that appears in the Old Testament spans a period of at least three hundred years. Since dating can be more precise when we think about when the prophets actually lived and worked (as opposed to when their words first appeared "in print"), we will date the prophetic books by the dates of the prophets.

Isaiah is probably the most well-known prophet with the most widely read words. The prophet Isaiah began his ministry "in the year that King Uzziah died," as we see in Isaiah 6:1, which was the year 742 B.C.E. In truth, the book of Isaiah is probably the product of three different authors/ prophets. The prophet Isaiah was responsible for chapters 1–39, chapters 40–55 come from a prophet who lived and worked during the time of the Babylonian exile (around

550 B.C.E.), and chapters 56–66 come from the time of the restoration (around 500 B.C.E.).

Jeremiah was called to his ministry during the reign of King Josiah (640–609 B.C.E.). According to Jeremiah 36, the prophet dictated his words to his scribe Baruch, who was responsible for keeping his message alive through his writings.

Lamentations appears immediately after the book of Jeremiah because the Latin Vulgate version of the Bible (prepared in 400 C.E.) added the words "of Jeremiah" to the title of the book. Lamentations consists of five poems, or dirges, in a 3+2 meter. The book was written by an unknown author who may have been an eyewitness to the fall of Jerusalem to the Babylonians in 587 B.C.E.

> Find the book of Lamentations, and read some of the poetry aloud using a 3+2 meter, in which the emphasis is always on the first phrase and the voice falls in the second phrase. (For example: HOW LONELY SITS THE CITY that once was full of people.) Does reading the text in that way help you see why the poems are called "Lamentations"?

The prophet Ezekiel was called to prophesy while in exile in Babylon (Ezek. 1:1–3). Using the death of his wife as a symbol, the prophet spoke of the destruction of Jerusalem and the effect of that event on the life of the people. Ezekiel's original words were recorded and expanded upon by an editor—perhaps a disciple—in the fifth century B.C.E.

After the book of Daniel (see below) we find the twelve minor prophets, so called because of their length (rather than the importance of their message). Here is a list of these prophets and their dates as best we know them. (All dates are B.C.E.)

> Hosea (750)
> Joel (300)
> Amos (755)
> Obadiah (587)
> Jonah (400)
> Micah (700)
> Nahum (625)
> Habakkuk (605)
> Zephaniah (630)
> Haggai (520)
> Zechariah (475)
> Malachi (460)

APOCALYPTIC LITERATURE

In between the book of Ezekiel and the twelve minor prophets, we find the book of Daniel, the only example of an apocalyptic book in the Old Testament. The word "apocalyptic" means "something hidden or covered up," and the name is attributed to Daniel because its language is mysterious and visionary, and is often purposely in code. There are hints of this kind of language in Ezekiel's prophecy, which explains why Daniel was located after Ezekiel in the canon.

The book of Daniel contains six stories and four visions, and in general it provides interpretations of history and predictions of the future. It was written by an anonymous author who wanted to attribute the writing to Daniel, who was an important person at the time (see Ezek. 14:14, where

Daniel is mentioned). This attribution ensured Daniel's inclusion in the canon.

When we turn the page from Malachi to Matthew, we cross a bridge that is about five hundred years long. But this bridge is a strong connection, nevertheless. Read the first verse of the Gospel of Matthew. How does it make the connection to the Old Testament?

THE GOSPELS

Whereas the span of years between the writing of the earliest and the latest of the Old Testament books was about eight hundred years, all twenty-seven books of the New Testament were written in a span of considerably less than one hundred years. The four Gospels (Matthew, Mark, Luke, and John), although they appear first in the order of books in the New Testament, were probably not the earliest books to be written.

The Gospels are basically biographies, portraying the life and times of Jesus. Each Gospel writer tells the life of Jesus in his own unique way, with a different emphasis that becomes clear from reading the Gospel. The Gospel of Mark was the first to be written, and Matthew and Luke were based in part on Mark. Matthew, Mark, and Luke are called the Synoptic Gospels. The word "synoptic" means "in common." The Gospel of John stands apart because of its theological (rather than biographical) character and message.

Matthew was written sometime between 75 and 100 C.E. by an unknown author. Some of the words in this Gospel probably originated with the apostle Matthew, and a later collector added to them. The Gospel of Matthew emphasizes Jesus as the fulfillment of the Old Testament law and promise.

Mark was the earliest Gospel to be written (around 65 C.E.) and was probably the work of the John Mark mentioned in Acts 15:37. This Gospel carries a special emphasis on the deeds and accomplishments of Jesus, portraying him as always on the move.

> Page through the Gospel of Mark, and note how many times the writer uses the word "immediately." You will be able to see the writer's portrayal of Jesus as a person of action.

The writer of Luke emphasizes Jesus as the caretaker of marginalized and downtrodden people. This Gospel was probably written by Luke the physician, who was, according to Colossians 4:14, a friend of Paul. The date of Luke is 80–85 C.E.

The Gospel of John was written by John the apostle or his disciple in 90–100 C.E. John's special emphasis is on the mystery of the divine/human Jesus.

History

The book of Acts traces the history of the early Christian church using the central figure of Paul. Acts continues the narrative begun in the Gospel of Luke and was written by the same author. There is a distinct geographical organization to Acts, with the church beginning in Jerusalem and spreading out through the Mediterranean and eventually as far as Rome.

LETTERS

The New Testament contains twenty-one letters, most of them written by Paul. In fact, some letters are attributed to Paul but probably were not written by him. Such attributions were common practice in the ancient world, where the concept of copyright was as yet unknown.

> We have seen this phenomenon various times, in which a certain biblical book is attributed to a famous person in order to give it more credibility. Would you consider attributing a work you authored to a more famous person? Why, or why not? How well would this practice work today?

Here is a list of all the New Testament letters, when they were written, and by whom. Remember that much of this information is necessarily conjecture.

Romans: written by Paul in 55 C.E.
First Corinthians: written by Paul in 52 C.E.
Second Corinthians: written by Paul in 55 C.E.
Galatians: written by Paul in 55 C.E.
Ephesians: written by Paul in 62 C.E.
Philippians: written by Paul in 58 C.E.
Colossians: written by Paul in 62 C.E.
First Thessalonians: written by Paul in 52 C.E.
Second Thessalonians: written by Paul in 53 C.E.
First Timothy: written by a disciple of Paul (date unknown)
Second Timothy: written by a disciple of Paul (date unknown)
Titus: written by a disciple of Paul (date unknown)
Philemon: written by Paul in 62 C.E.

Hebrews: written by an anonymous author in 65 C.E.
James: written by an unknown author in 90 C.E.
First Peter: written by an unknown author in 65 C.E.
Second Peter: written by a disciple of Peter in 110 C.E.
First John: written by an anonymous author in 90 C.E.
Second John: written by an anonymous author in 90 C.E.
Third John: written by an anonymous author in 90 C.E.
Jude: written by an anonymous author in 80 C.E.

We have skimmed through a whole section of material that is rich with theological themes and history. For more information on each of these letters, consult a commentary or Bible dictionary. Or better yet, read the letters themselves. In a good study Bible, you will be able to read a short introduction before each letter.

Apocalyptic Literature

The book of Revelation is similar to the book of Daniel in the Old Testament, with its visions about history and the eventual consummation of human history. Like Daniel, Revelation was written to encourage those who were being persecuted—in this case, the persecution was coming from the Roman emperor Domitian (81–96 C.E.). Revelation was written by an unknown author by the name of John, who had been exiled to the island of Patmos.

Recall the first session that discussed the concept of canon. Now that you have had a chance to familiarize yourself with the canon, or contents, of the Bible, what is your own canon? That is, what are the books you feel most comfortable with? Everyone has a "canon within the canon." What is yours? Take a few minutes to compare yours with others in the group.

FIVE

Bible Tools and Translations

INTRODUCTION

To prepare for this lesson, scour your bookshelves and the shelves in your church's library for various resources such as Bible commentaries, concordances, dictionaries, and different Bible translations. Bring them with you to the study group, along with your favorite translation of the Bible.

In the recent survey mentioned previously in this study, members of the United Church of Christ were asked whether or not they agreed with the following statement: The Bible is hard to understand. Almost two-thirds of the respondents agreed with this statement. And when asked whether the Bible was important in their lives, approximately 95 percent of respondents answered that the Bible was either somewhat important or very important in their lives. Taken together, what do these two responses indicate? Talk with your group about these answers.

In today's session we will familiarize ourselves with basic Bible tools and how to use them. Of course, not all these resources are absolutely necessary in order to discuss and appreciate any particular biblical passage. In fact, you can have fascinating and revealing discussions just by reading a passage in various translations and discussing the differences you find.

However, most of us are not Bible scholars, and we approach the Bible with a certain innocence and lack of background. Sometimes the Bible is simply difficult to understand because the language and concepts are no longer in use or are shadowed by layers of theology and interpretation. Sometimes we need to unlearn earlier ideas or look at a passage with new eyes. Tools such as the ones that we will examine today can help us with these kinds of new understandings.

BIBLE TRANSLATIONS

We often use the term "translation" to refer to a particular version of the Bible, but actually, there are three categories of versions and each has its own characteristics. When we are deciding which version of the Bible to use, it helps to know whether we are talking about a translation, a dynamic equivalency, or a paraphrase.

Translations are literal renderings from Hebrew (for the Old Testament) or Greek (for the New Testament) into a language such as English. Examples of translations include the following:

The King James Version (published in England in 1611)
The American Standard Version (American version of the King James Version, published in 1901)
The Revised Standard Version (a revision of the American Standard Version, published in the mid-1900s)

The New English Bible (published in Scotland in 1961 [New Testament] and 1970 [Old Testament])

The Jerusalem Bible (translated by French Roman Catholic scholars and published in English in 1966)

The New International Version (published by the Christian Reformed Church in the mid-1970s)

The New Revised Standard Version (a newer version of the Revised Standard Version, published in 1989, updated for inclusive language and recent learnings from the discovery of the Dead Sea Scrolls)

Dynamic equivalencies are different from literal translations in that scholars attempt to render the original Hebrew and Greek in language that is more contemporary. The goal is to create the same context for readers today that was created in the original language(s) for the original readers. An example of a dynamic equivalent rendering would be translating the original "a sabbath day's journey" as "about half a mile." This rendering is not a literal translation, but gives the meaning of the original in more contemporary terms. The best-known example of a dynamic equivalency is the Good News Bible, also know as Today's English Version. It was published in 1966 under the auspices of the American Bible Society.

Paraphrases are different from both literal translations and dynamic equivalencies in that they take more liberties with the original text in order to make the Bible understandable to contemporary readers. While paraphrasing a text, the author makes decisions along the way about how the original might be better understandable. Let's look at an example from a well-known paraphrase—the Living Bible, published in 1971. Daniel 3:5 reads as follows in the New Revised Standard Version: "When you hear the sound of the horn, pipe, lyre, trigon, harp, drum, and entire musical ensemble." The Living Bible combines all these musical instruments into "the band." When you are using a paraphrase, it is helpful to know when the author is making judgments and when the author is providing a literal translation, but this is rarely obvious. It is probably best to use a paraphrase along with a more literal translation and compare the two renderings as you read.

> Try writing your own paraphrases of a few of your favorite verses. Or select a verse or two for each person to paraphrase in his or her own way, and then share the paraphrases among your group. In that way you will better understand the process of paraphrasing and the various decisions that need to be made along the way.

> What is your favorite version of the Bible? Is it a translation, a dynamic equivalency, or a paraphrase? (If your favorite is not among those listed above, look in the preface or introduction to your Bible.) Why is this particular version your favorite?

Of course, even the most literal translations are one step away from the original Greek or Hebrew. The translator always has a number of options from which to choose in translating a particular word, for example, just as we often can choose from a number of words when we want to convey a particular idea or thought. How do we choose? Sometimes from our memory bank of favorite words. When in doubt, we may use a dictionary. And that is what the translators did as well. The result is a variety of perspectives, and some will make more sense than others. Let's look at one verse and the various ways it has been translated in some of our English versions of the Bible.

Open your own Bible, and find Lamentations 1:1. This verse appears in various translations as follows:

How solitary lies the city, once so full of people!
Once great among nations, now become a widow;
once queen among provinces, now put to forced labour!
(New English Bible)

How lonely lies Jerusalem, once so full of people!
Once honored by the world, she is now like a widow;
The noblest of cities has fallen into slavery.
(Today's English Version)

How lonely sits the city
that was full of people!
How like a widow she has become,
she that was great among the nations!
She that was a princess among the cities
has become a vassal.
(Revised Standard Version)

How doth the city sit solitary, that was full of people!
How is she become as a widow! She that was great among the nations, and princess among the provinces, how is she become tributary!
(King James Version)

Oh, how lonely she sits,
   the city once thronged with people,
as if suddenly widowed.
   Though once great among the nations,
she, the princess among provinces,
   is now reduced to vassalage.

(Jerusalem Bible)

How lonely sits the city
   that once was full of people!
How like a widow she has become,
   she that was great among the nations!
She that was a princess among the provinces
    has become a vassal.

(New Revised Standard Version)

If you have a number of different translations available, take a few minutes to look up a few favorite verses, and read them aloud, comparing different versions. Then discuss what you learned from this exercise. Have you changed your mind about which version is your favorite? Why, or why not?

STUDY BIBLES

Study Bibles are available in various translations—most often the New International Version, the King James Version, the Revised Standard Version, and the New Revised Standard Version. One well-known example of a study Bible is the Oxford Annotated Bible, published in the Revised Standard Version and the New Revised Standard Version by Oxford University Press. This and other study Bibles contain the basic biblical text in one of the versions, plus added benefits such as explanatory notes, general articles, and an introduction to each biblical book giving information about date, contents, and authorship.

> If you have a study Bible available, look up the Lamentations passage, and see what information the notes provide. Also skim the introduction to Lamentations for background information on the book.

Concordances

Bible concordances come in many sizes and types. A concordance can be as simple and brief as a list of words in the back of a study Bible, arranged index style, with chapter and verse references. This listing would correspond to the content index in the back of a book and is not complete. A concordance can also be as complex as a lengthy volume that catalogues every single usage of every single word in the Bible. One example is *Strong's Exhaustive Concordance of the Bible*, published by a number of different publishers and based on different versions of the Bible. Of course, complete concordances like this must be keyed to a certain translation of the Bible, since different words may be used to translate the same verse. Often if the meaning of a particular word is obscure, discovering how the same word is used in other passages can shed light on its meaning in the passage you are working with.

> Select a word from Lamentations 1:1, and find it in a concordance if you have one available. Now look up some or all of the other passages in which that word is used.

Take note of the various contexts in which the word is used, How does this exercise help you better understand the meaning of the Wuid you chose? If you have time, look up other words from some of your favorite verses.

BIBLE DICTIONARIES

Using a Bible dictionary is often a quicker way to discern the meaning of a word than looking it up in a concordance. A dictionary will provide the various meanings of a word and tie the meanings to specific verses in the Bible. In the case of the word "widow," for example, a dictionary might indicate that at times the word is used in its literal sense (such as in the story of the widow's mite) and at times the meaning is metaphorical or symbolic (as in the Lamentations passage, where it refers to the solitary state of the city of Jerusalem).

Biblical dictionaries function much like our English-language dictionaries. They can be compact and cover the basic uses of certain key words, or they can be multivolume sets that cover both common and uncommon terms, proper names, place names, and so forth.

If you have a dictionary available, look up one of the words you examined in the last exercise. Did you find any additional information in the dictionary that you did not learn from using a concordance?

COMMENTARIES

Bible commentaries give verse-by-verse explanations of biblical passages. As is the case with dictionaries and concordances, commentaries can vary from small, paper-back volumes that provide material in an overview fashion to multivolume sets that provide detailed information, sometimes of a technical nature. Perhaps the most well-known multivolume commentary series is the *Abingdon Interpreter's Bible*, originally published in the 1950s and now being published in a revised form at the rate of about two volumes per year.

> If you have a commentary or commentaries available, look up Lamentations 1:1. You are likely to find some or all of the following information.

Lamentations 1:1 and the following verses are set as poetry in biblical Hebrew, and the meter is that of a dirge. You can almost feel the dirgelike quality of the meter if you read it aloud with the emphasis on the first phrase and not on the second:

HOW LONELY SITS THE CITY that once was full of people!

The poems in Lamentations are mostly acrostic in nature. That is, verse 1 begins with the first letter of the Hebrew alphabet (the Hebrew word for "how" begins with an "aleph"), verse 2 with the second letter, and so on.

"The city" refers to Jerusalem, which was devastated some years earlier by the Babylonian invasion and captivity.

> You might want to look up some of your favorite verses in the commentaries you have on hand.

Your Own Mind and Heart, and Your Collective Wisdom

In a sense, we have saved the best for last. Remember that Bible tools such as commentaries, dictionaries, and paraphrases are the products of human endeavor and therefore are not perfect or error free. After using the various tools mentioned here, you will have a better sense of what the text means. Now you can take the final step of discerning what *you* think it means. Trust the experts (as we do in fields such as law and medicine), but make the final determinations in your own heart and mind.

And do not forget the value of collective wisdom. The more you discuss questions and concerns related to a specific passage with others in your Bible study group, the more clarity you will achieve. No, you will not always agree on the meaning of a passage. But as you will see when you read various commentaries, neither do the scholars.

Pronunciation Guide

Here are suggested pronunciations for some of the terms used in this study book:

Agur: ah-GOOR
Apocalypse: ah-PAH-cuh-lips
Apocalyptic: ah-pah-cuh-LIP-
   tic
Apocrypha: ah-PAH-crah-fah
Deuteronomistic: doo-ter-ah-
   no-MIS-tic
Essenes: ESS-eens
Habakkuk: hah-BAA-cook
Haggai: HAG-eye
Hapax legomena: hah-pocks-
   leh-GAH-meh-nah
Hezekiah: heh-zeh-KIGH-ah
Hieroglyphics: high-roh-
   GLIF-ics

Jamnia: JAM-nee-ah
Judean: joo-DEE-an
Lemuel: LEM-yoo-el
Malachi: MAL-eh-kigh
Masoretes: MASS-or-eets
Nahum: NAY-hum
Obadiah: oh-bah-DIGH-ah
Origen: ORE-ih-gen
Pentateuch: PEN-tah-tuke
Qoheleth: koh-HELL-eth
Qumran: koom-RAHN
Synoptic: sin-OP-tic
Torah: TOR-ah
Zechariah: zak-ah-RIGH-ah
Zephaniah: zef-ah-NIGH-ah